HOW IS A
BICYCLE MADE?

BY HENRY HORENSTEIN

SIMON & SCHUSTER BOOKS FOR YOUNG READERS

Published by Simon & Schuster
New York London Toronto Sydney Tokyo Singapore

My special thanks to the many people who made this book happen, in particular Mary Zellmer, Dick Moran, Jeff Grotjahn, and Peter St. Onge at TREK and all the people at the TREK factory in Waterloo, WI. Casimir Domalewski handled the lighting chores on location and Peggy Thomson helped after the fact. Jim DaSilva and Jeff Johnston of Laughing Alley Bicycle Shop in Allston, MA and Charlie McCorkel and Mark Plaut of Bicycle Habitat in New York City, Bill Wilkinson of the Bicycle Institute of America, Janice Wilhite of the Bicycle Manufacturer's Association of America, and John Auer were also generous. Valorie Fisher and Lawson Little helped make the cover photo work, Richard Maurer, Jacquie and Roy Strasburger, Marco Steinsieck, and Faith Hamlin were all very helpful. Thanks also to Frezzolini Severance Design, Westerly, RI; Pam Pollack, David Neuhaus, Lucille Chomowicz, and Theresa Gaffney at Simon & Schuster. And, as usual, Tracy Hill helped in too many ways to list.

SIMON & SCHUSTER BOOKS FOR YOUNG READERS
Simon & Schuster Building, Rockefeller Center,
1230 Avenue of the Americas, New York, New York 10020.
Designed by Sylvia Frezzolini.
The text for this book was set in 14 point Baskerville.
Manufactured in the United States of America

10 9 8 7 6 5 4 3 2 1

Library of Congress Cataloging-in-Publication Data
Horenstein, Henry.   How is a bicycle made?/by Henry Horenstein.
Summary: Describes the construction and function of various parts of a bicycle and how they are combined into a finished product.
1. Bicycles—Design and construction—Juvenile literature.
[1. Bicycles and bicycling—Design and construction.] I. Title.
TL410.H67   1993   629.227'.2—dc20
CIP   92-25375
ISBN 0-671-77749-1

This book is for Tracy Hill,
the sainted one

Imagine yourself on a bicycle, your legs pumping the pedals until you can coast along freely, with the wind streaming through your hair. You may remember learning how to balance on your first two-wheeler. You probably own a bicycle now. But have you ever wondered just how a bicycle is made?

A bicycle has about 300 parts. When you think of a bicycle, the wheels may be what come to mind first, but bicycle making actually begins with the frame. A frame has to be strong because all the other parts of the bicycle attach to it. This is why frames are made of sturdy materials, such as steel or aluminum and carbon fiber. Because aluminum is somewhat lighter in weight than the other materials, most racing bikes are made of aluminum. Most kids' bikes, like the one you ride, are made of steel.

Frame making begins with long tubes that are joined together with smaller connecting pieces which are specially formed and shaped to fit precisely and securely.

Steel bicycle tubes are joined in a process called brazing which bonds them securely. This is done by melting solder, a special metal alloy, around the joints where the parts connect. The brazing is done by hand with a gas-fueled torch,

or on an assembly line where the heat is provided by electricity.

Aluminum and carbon fiber tubes and parts can't be heated because the material is too sensitive. Instead, they are joined with a special glue called epoxy. You may have used epoxy to build plastic models.

The type of epoxy used in bicycle making is so strong that it's also used to construct airplanes and spaceships.

Glued frames are put on a press-up table, where all the parts are pressed together by a powerful hydraulic machine. Then the frame is put into a 150°F. oven for an hour to harden the epoxy bond.

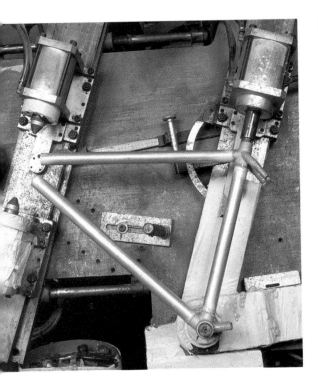

A bicycle frame must be straight in order for the bicycle to ride smoothly, so each frame is carefully checked and double-checked on an alignment table. Laser beams are focused on the frame, and the shadow of the frame is measured to see that it falls in the right place. If the frame is not straight, it must be rejoined.

Completed frames are thoroughly cleaned before they are painted. Steel frames are sandblasted to remove large particles of sediment. Then they are dipped into a series of tanks. The first contains acid; the second, water; and the third, an antirust chemical.

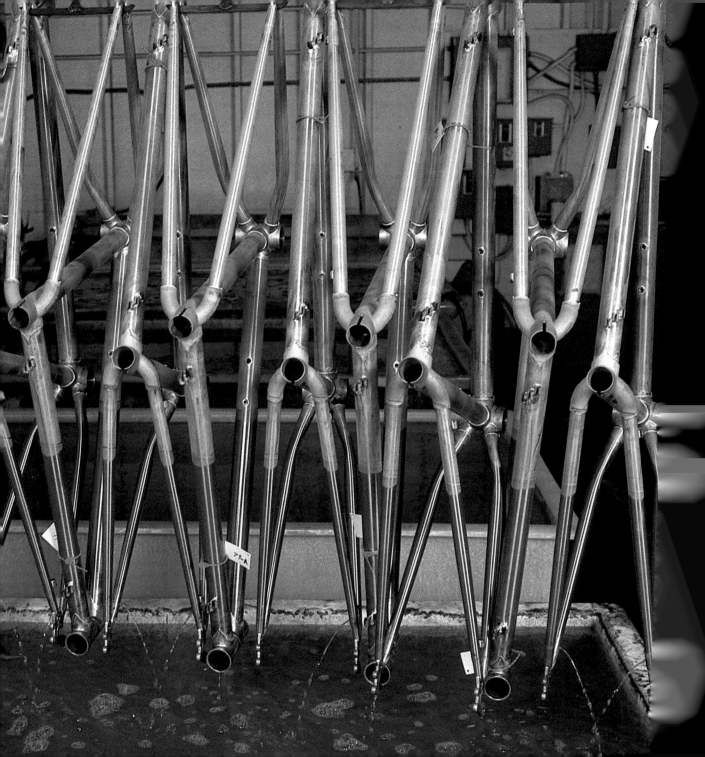

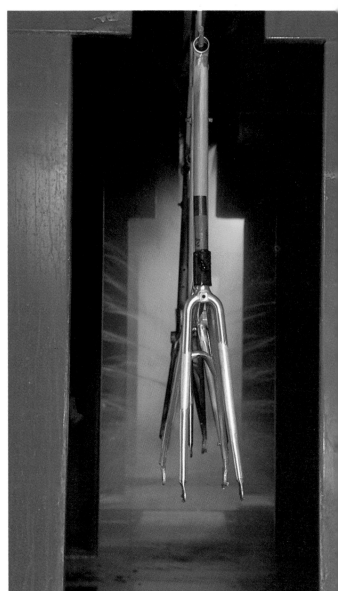

Aluminum and carbon fiber frames are sent through a machine similar to a car wash, where high-pressure jets of water remove all dirt and grit.

Painting begins with the corners and other hard-to-reach places. Workers spray these spots by hand and then send the frames through an automatic painting booth, where the frame receives two complete coats. After each coat of paint is applied, the frame travels on a conveyor belt through an oven to "cure," or dry, the paint.

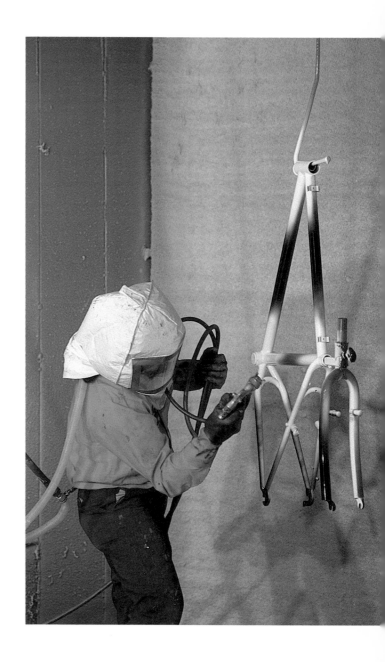

Decals are soaked in a tub of water and applied by hand to the painted frames. The frames then move through another painting booth, where they receive a finishing coat of a hard, clear sealer to protect the paint and decals from scratching or other damage.

While the frame is being assembled and painted, the wheels are also being constructed. A bicycle wheel consists of a lightweight metal rim, a tire, wire spokes, and a small rotating hub in the center.

Wheel assembly begins with the rim. The rim has a hole for each spoke, and a machine reinforces the holes with rivets. The number of spokes, between twenty-eight and thirty-six, depends on the type of bicycle. Touring bikes, which have to carry heavy loads, have the most spokes for reinforcement. . Racing bikes, which have to be as lightweight as possible, have the fewest.

The spokes are carefully inserted into the hub at the center of the wheel and then attached to the rim in a crisscross pattern. This process is called lacing because of the way the woven wires resemble laced shoelaces. Lacing can be done by hand or by machine.

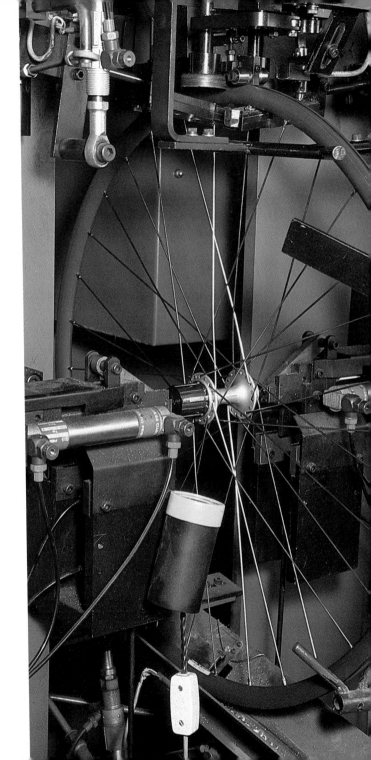

It is important for the spokes to be just the right tension. Metal fasteners, inserted by machine through the rim holes, attach the spokes firmly to the rim. Then each spoke is tightened by machine.

Finally, a rubber inner tube and tire are stretched around the rim. When the tire is inflated, the wheel will be ready to roll.

The last unit to be assembled at the factory is the one that makes the whole bicycle go. This is the power train. The power train consists of the pedals, the front and rear sprockets, and the chain. A sprocket is a metal wheel with cogs, or "teeth." When you pedal a bicycle, the pedals turn the sprocket on the front wheel, which moves the chain, which turns the rear wheel sprocket, which turns the rear wheel; and this makes the bicycle go.

Sprockets are attached by hand to the hub, the center part of the wheel, by a process called threading. Then the back wheel is inserted into the frame, and a chain is run around the sprockets.

The movement of the chain between the sprockets determines the gear positions of the bicycle, such as high gear or low gear. A one-speed bicycle has one front and one rear sprocket. Multispeed bicycles, however, have many sprockets, and each position is a different gear. Large sprockets are used in the easy-to-turn low gears. Small sprockets are used in the hard-to-turn high gears.

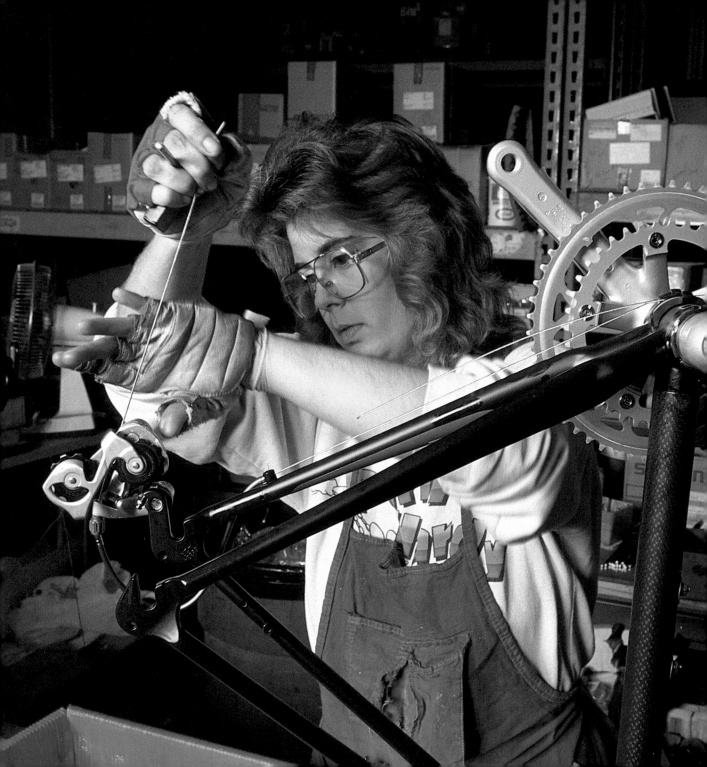

The chain is moved between different sprockets and into different gears by derailleurs. This part makes it harder or easier to pedal the bicycle. There is one derailleur for the front and another for the back. Derailleurs are operated by wire cables that are already attached to the frame.

Although the bicycle is not quite ready to ride, the factory work is now completed. The bicycle is boxed and shipped to local stores.

At the bicycle store, several parts are added to complete the assembly. These include pedals, handlebars, shift levers for the gears, brakes, reflectors, seat post, and saddle. These things are not attached at the factory, because some of these parts, such as the pedals and handlebars, would make the frame too bulky to fit into the box easily. Pieces such as brakes and reflectors could shift and even break off during shipping.

Most importantly, each bicycle needs to be carefully adjusted to fit the rider, so saddles and handlebars are added in the store, where you can try them out and the necessary adjustments can be made. Each bicycle is fine-tuned to correct anything that may have shifted during shipping. Spokes are loosened or tightened, brake pads and gears are adjusted, and the front wheel is attached and aligned.

Finally, the bicycle is ready to ride. Happy cycling!